THIS IS ME

1001
QUESTIONS TO LEARN MORE ABOUT YOURSELF

chartwell
books

THIS JOURNAL BELONGS TO...

Kathleen

CONTENTS

HOW TO USE

• • •

Aristotle once wrote, "Knowing yourself is the beginning of all wisdom." Filling the pages of this journal is tantamount to jumping into a pool full of wisdom. We're living in the Information Age, and it might feel like there's a barrage of information coming our way all the time. Yet, what's missing from the fountains of information is information about ourselves. It's vital knowledge that can affect how we deal and cope with the world around us.

How to use this collection of prompts is relatively easy. If you can, consider it part of your morning and/or bedtime routines. The main objective is to find a way to incorporate it into your day. If you can't do that, then keep it handy for when you feel ready. Keep it close by.

Each section is made to understand a part of yourself more. *About Me* will explore your personal tastes—likes and dislikes. *A Little History* will inform all you've seen and lived through. *The Present is a Present* will have you looking at your surroundings and taking stock of all you have right in front of you. *Looking Forward to the Future* will have you setting goals and imagining the kind of life you've dreamt of having.

You may begin to feel different. You may start to see things in new ways. You may feel more vulnerable. You may feel lighter than you've ever felt before. These result from you interacting with yourself and unloading some of the things you may have never unloaded onto a piece of paper. Enjoy this time. Open yourself up to learning more about yourself and answering some questions honestly.

There are many ways to use this collection. You can share tidbits with someone close, or you can keep it all to yourself. Ultimately, *This is Me* is a guide...of yourself, so welcome to the beginning.

ABOUT ME

"To be yourself
in a world that is
constantly trying to
make you something
else is the greatest
accomplishment."

–RALPH WALDO EMERSON

1. What is your happiest memory from childhood?

2. What mementos of the past have you kept over the years?

3. Do you consider yourself to be self-confident?

4. What is your relationship with self-confidence?

5. Have you ever had a second home?

6. What's your favorite way to travel? Car, train, or plane?

7. When was the last time you were told of your shortcomings?

8. Do you have any habits that are both good and bad?

9. What is something you've wanted but realized that you didn't need?

10. What was elementary school like for you?

11. What was middle school like for you?

12. What was high school like for you?

13. What is one thing you need to do every day?

14. Do you like being in romantic relationships?

15. What do you value most in a friendship?

16. What does a best friend mean to you?

17. Who is your best friend?

18. To whom are you the most dependable person?

19. How are you feeling in this very moment?

20. Are you an outdoors kind of person?

21. What's your favorite drink to sip on when socializing?

22. Do you know how to use power tools?

23. What's the one thing you don't mind doing step by step?

24. What's a photograph you always have to have near you?

25. Do you like to dance?

26. Would people you know describe you as accommodating?

27. What would you describe as beautiful?

28. What would you describe as ugly?

29. What do you consider to be rude?

30. What does the concept of soulmates mean to you?

31. What's the house chore you dislike the most?

32. What sound do you dislike the most?

33. What sound do you like the most?

34. What smell do you dislike the most?

35. What smell do you like the most?

36. How do you believe people fall in love?

37. Do you believe in "the one"?

38. What's your favorite spread? Peanut butter or jelly?

39. How do you blow off steam?

40. What do you prefer? The heat or the cold?

41. Do you consider yourself to be a faithful person?

42. What song do you always skip?

43. When are you most cooperative?

44. What is your favorite color?

45. What is your favorite ice cream flavor?

46. What is your favorite candy flavor?

47. What's your favorite month of the year?

48. What's your favorite day of the year?

49. Do you consider yourself to be a good driver?

50. Do you love yourself?

51. What do you do when you get the hiccups?

52. What is something that always takes your breath away?

53. What is something that doesn't affect you but affects others?

54. Do you do anything to ensure you get a good night's rest?

55. What's your main source of stress-relief?

56. What is something you will always defend?

57. Who is someone you will always defend?

58. Do you like to argue?

59. How would you describe the truth?

60. Do you consider yourself to be assertive?

61. Is there a song that reminds you of happy times?

62. What will always make you laugh?

63. What are you the perfect mixture of?

64. Who's the first person you would thank during an acceptance speech?

65. What's your biggest pet peeve?

66. What is the one thing that can always cheer you up?

67. What time in the day do you feel most productive?

68. What's your favorite cuisine?

69. If you were a dish, what kind of dish would it be?

70. What kind of animal would you be?

71. What's your favorite breakfast food?

72. Are you a light packer?

73. Dogs or cats?

74. What is the one grocery item you must always get?

75. Are you someone who enjoys traveling?

76. Where have you traveled to that personifies your best qualities?

77. Where is one place you would never go to again?

78. Do you think joy and happiness are the same thing?

79. Do you enjoy watching television?

80. What's a sport you can always watch?

81. What is always easy for you to pay attention to?

82. Do you like the spotlight?

83. What is your favorite musical genre?

84. Do you like going to the dentist?

85. Is there something you would outlaw if you could?

86. What's your favorite snack?

87. Are you good at reading maps?

88. Are you a rollercoaster person or a Ferris wheel person?

89. Does the idea of permanence appeal to you?

90. What is one thing from your home you prize most?

91. How do you like to dress when you go out?

92. What's a story you constantly tell yourself?

93. Who balances you?

94. What do you believe everyone should have?

95. How do you deal with disappointment?

96. Beer or wine?

97. Stick or automatic?

98. What's your nightly routine before bed?

99. What's your favorite part of grooming?

100. What's your personal lifeline?

101. What do you complain about the most?

102. What do you always argue about with people?

103. What is your signature gift for others?

104. How do you show people you care?

105. Do you consider yourself to be a thoughtful person?

106. Do you believe in miracles?

107. What kind of person deserves your love and affection?

108. What is your favorite photo of yourself?

109. What would your catchphrase be?

110. What is your least favorite photo of yourself?

111. Are you good at showing emotions?

112. What are boundaries you consistently set for yourself?

113. What do you love most about your best friend?

114. Do you have what it takes to be a teacher?

115. Do you lose things often?

116. What are people always surprised to find out about you?

117. Who is someone you've always wanted to impress?

118. Who is someone you go to when you get bad news?

119. Are you a people person?

120. What's your favorite game to play?

121. Are you quick to apologize?

122. What is your favoriting thing to wear?

123. What's the one food you can't live without?

124. Would you ever forgive someone for lying to you?

125. Are you good at first impressions?

126. Do you like wearing the color black?

127. Do you like wearing the color white?

128. If you were to get a tattoo, what would it be of?

129. What's a kind of clothing you would never buy?

130. Are you attracted to charismatic people?

131. Do you think charisma is a skill or quality?

132. How do you channel compassion?

133. Do you consider yourself to be unique?

134. What is your favorite TV show?

135. Has there ever been a song that has made you cry?

136. Do you consider yourself to be lucky?

137. What's your favorite kind of leftover to have?

138. Do you believe in God?

139. Who is the person you've always gotten along with?

140. Do you believe that ignorance is bliss?

141. Do you like sports?

142. Do you consider yourself to be a responsible person?

143. How are you when the doctor gives you a shot?

144. Describe yourself in three words.

145. What is the one thing you always have to spare?

146. What is something you believe can only be done one way?

147. What are your views on gender?

148. Are you good with babies?

149. How would you describe real love?

150. How would you describe fake love?

151. Is there something you just can't bring yourself to believe?

152. What advice do you usually give people?

153. Is there a façade you maintain?

154. Do you get asked to present your ID often?

155. What's more important? Trust or respect?

156. Would people describe you as being gentle as a lamb?

157. What's the most important thing to humanity?

158. Are you afraid of spiders?

159. Do you always deliver what you promise?

160. Do you believe in life beyond the grave?

161. Do the majority of your actions denote affection?

162. Coffee or tea?

163. Is there a limit you set for yourself on things?

164. Do you spill secrets?

165. What's a message you would broadcast to the entire planet?

166. What's the first clue a person will come through?

167. Why do you think burials are so important to humans?

168. What is your definition of elegance?

169. What happens in the present day that you consider medieval?

170. Where do you go for insight when you're problem solving?

171. Do you like mushrooms in your food?

172. What do you consider to be pure?

173. Is disappointment prevalent in your life?

174. What's the real glitch in the matrix?

175. How often do you look at the clock?

176. Do you consider yourself to be a straight-shooter?

177. How easy do things come to you?

178. Is dignity important?

179. Do you like to listen to the radio?

180. Is there a particular way you like to do things?

181. Do you always aim high?

182. Do you have a favorite brand of soap?

183. What's the formula to make you happy?

184. What's your favorite kind of cake?

185. What is one food you can live without?

186. What does it take for you to have a blast?

187. What famous paintings would you put up in a gallery?

188. Have you ever been sailing?

189. Do you consider yourself to be gregarious?

190. Do you spend too much time on your computer?

191. Do you prefer the city or the country?

192. Are you a salad person?

193. Who has shattered your expectations?

194. Do you always have to be right?

195. Do you like when people use nicknames?

196. Are there conspiracy theories you think are true?

197. If it takes a village to raise a child, who's your village?

198. Is there a reluctance on your part to be great?

199. What does it mean to have personal agency?

200. How distant are your distant relatives?

201. When have you considered yourself to be a liability?

202. What stories usually make you shiver?

203. Do you typically become extra determined when someone doubts you?

204. What is your favorite sculpture?

205. When have you wrongly gotten second place?

206. Do you ever speak out loud when you're alone?

207. Would you ever willingly shave your head?

208. Is there a computer software you can't live without?

209. What's the one thing that should happen at every get-together?

210. Who is someone in your life that is super adaptable?

211. Do you admire when people are adaptable?

212. Make a list of three things that would describe a perfect day.

213. Have you ever felt shame?

214. If you could, which emotion would you bottle up and sell?

215. How do you get past feelings of shame?

216. Why do you think relationships deteriorate?

217. Do you keep a photo album?

218. What's a human characteristic that's essential to achieve success?

219. Does pleasure automatically make something bad?

220. Do you groan more for physical or mental frustrations?

221. What can someone walk away with after meeting you?

222. What are you a scholar of that isn't typically scholarly?

223. Is there an apparatus you think is funny to look at?

224. What is your definition of foolish?

225. Is there a song that always reminds you of nature?

226. Is visibility important when it comes to your ideal life?

227. What do you usually reveal to someone new?

228. What usually causes you to emotionally explode?

229. How early do you typically wake up in the morning?

230. Do you read often?

231. Do you consider yourself the wisest person in a room?

232. Is there an assumption no one should make about you?

233. Who in your life is prey to bad things?

234. Who is the most balanced person you know?

235. Do you spray or dab perfume or cologne?

236. Do you know how to swim?

237. What's a memory every kid should have?

238. What is your relationship to time?

239. What's in your hallway?

240. Are you a native of a place?

241. If you could put together a tribute to someone, who would it be?

242. Are you honest?

243. What is the one thing everyone should know about you?

244. What are you always interested in?

245. What is natural in you?

246. What confuses you?

247. What is a victory to you, and not to others?

248. What's your favorite dish that someone else cooks?

249. How do you express discontent?

250. Who is most similar to you?

251. What is a level of brilliance you aspire to?

A LITTLE
HISTORY

"Till this moment I never knew myself."

– JANE AUSTEN

252. When was the last time you were sad?

253. What do you think people first notice when they meet you?

254. Who do you wish you had apologized to?

255. Who do you wish had apologized to you?

256. What did you like most about school?

257. What is your favorite song?

258. What was your favorite book as a child?

259. What was your favorite book as an adult?

260. What was your first kiss like?

261. What is the one thing you will always say "no" to?

262. Has someone ever betrayed you?

263. What is your favorite way to listen to music?

264. What was the last moment you felt ashamed?

265. What's your earliest memory?

266. If you wrote an autobiography, what would you name it?

267. What was your favorite place to study in school?

268. What's the biggest scandal you ever witnessed?

269. What was something you used to hate having for dinner?

270. What's the most rebellious thing you've ever done?

271. When's the last time you felt anything close to ecstasy?

272. Have you always been an active person?

273. Did you have an imaginary friend growing up?

274. What has been the most critical event in your life?

275. Who was your favorite elementary school teacher?

276. Who was your favorite middle school teacher?

277. Who was your favorite high school teacher?

278. Have you ever experienced a violation of privacy?

279. Have you ever patched things up with someone?

280. What's the last wedding you went to?

281. What's a first-hand experience you have that no one else has?

282. Have you ever pleaded to someone to do something?

283. How have you felt when you realized you needed something?

284. Is there a story of you in the wilderness?

285. Who in your life would you describe as soft as silk?

286. What's the hugest house you've been in?

287. Do you journal?

288. Is there a place that always reminds you of someone?

289. When's the last time you had to take a walk?

290. What's the tensest situation you've ever been in?

291. How has your reflection changed over the years?

292. What's something you never wanted to be responsible for?

293. Have you ever ignored your instincts about something?

294. What's something you liked to wear when you were younger?

295. Have you ever seen a bolt of lightning hit the ground?

296. Do you consider yourself to be a good student?

297. What's your favorite memory in the snow?

298. What's your favorite summer memory?

299. How has your taste in entertainment changed over time?

300. How has your taste in entertainment not changed over time?

301. Has anyone ever forced their way into your heart?

302. When was the last time you saw a beautiful sunset?

303. What's your relationship with failure?

304. Have you ever felt judgmental toward someone?

305. Who are your core group of friends?

306. What is something you were afraid of before but aren't today?

307. What's been your experience in romance?

308. Has anyone ever given you flowers?

309. Have you given anyone flowers?

310. What's a movie you know by heart?

311. What's a song you know by heart?

312. Have you ever been confused for someone else?

313. What was your favorite toy when you were young?

314. When have you been the readiest?

315. Have you ever been in love?

316. Have you ever confessed to something you didn't do?

317. Have you ever confessed to something you did do?

318. Is there an experience you would label as "bland"?

319. Did you ever have a security blanket when you were growing up?

320. Was there a stuffed animal you carried around constantly when you were a child?

321. Have you ever been chased?

322. Have you ever chased someone?

323. When was the last time you went to a party?

324. Have you ever been apathetic toward someone?

325. When's the last time you were sick?

326. Have you ever looked back and regretted being stubborn?

327. Have you ever been jealous of someone?

328. Have you ever felt used by someone else?

329. How do you describe your past relationships?

330. When's the last time you felt protective over someone?

331. When were you at your best?

332. What would you choose as your funniest moment?

333. Have you ever experienced severe weather?

334. Have you ever been scared for your life?

335. What's the last lie you told?

336. What's the most irresponsible thing you've ever seen someone do?

337. Have you ever consoled someone?

338. Who has believed in you when you were at your lowest?

339. Have you ever left a party early?

340. What has made you proud?

341. What was the spark for your biggest inspiration?

342. What's your most memorable birthday?

343. What's a situation you replay in your head often?

344. What's the last thing you've won?

345. Who is someone you've impressed?

346. What did you hate most about school?

347. Is there a rumor about yourself that has shocked you?

348. Who is the first person you call with good news?

349. Have you ever walked barefoot on the grass?

350. Have you ever hurt someone's feelings and didn't mean to?

351. Have you ever meant to hurt someone's feelings?

352. What's a prevalent trend in your childhood?

353. What's a memory you have at a playground?

354. Is there a person you've let lie to you?

355. Have you ever left someone behind?

356. When's the last time you felt lonely?

357. Have you ever willingly wasted someone's time?

358. Has someone ever willingly wasted your time?

359. What is the worst idea you ever had?

360. Is there someone you don't get along with anymore?

361. Has there been a moment you've given your all?

362. What's the worst mistake you've ever made?

363. Who was your first crush?

364. Have you ever prayed?

365. What's the easiest thing you've ever done?

366. What was your favorite Saturday morning cartoon?

367. When's the last time you experienced sweltering heat?

368. When's the last time you were really, really cold?

369. Have you ever been thrust into a situation unprepared?

370. Have you ever been physically exhausted?

371. Is there anything in your life that you'd describe as "ephemeral"?

372. Where were you the last time you got a mosquito bite?

373. Was there an instance you remember running manically?

374. Have you ever been ice skating?

375. What has been an event that has been favorable?

376. What makes you think of the phrase, "It's always darkest before the dawn"?

377. How did you feel the last time someone insulted you?

378. What is your visual perspective when you see someone hurt?

379. Who have you pardoned in your life without them knowing?

380. Have you ever confused someone with someone else?

381. When was the last time you were with someone?

382. Have you ever researched something and were pleasantly surprised?

383. Did you ever feel pressure to complete a project?

384. Have you ever combined cereals?

385. Did you realize something wasn't actually worth your time?

386. Have you ever carried the torch for someone?

387. What used to be your favorite quote?

388. What's a chapter you had no issue closing in your life?

389. What's a prevalent trend in your teenage years?

390. Have you experienced something you would call an adventure?

391. What was a metaphorical parachute in your life once?

392. What habit did you get rid of pretty fast?

393. What was something you wrongly counted as a win?

394. What is something you have cut out of your life?

395. Do you remember a time when someone towered over you?

396. When's the last time you enjoyed a continental breakfast?

397. Have you ever changed a spare tire?

398. What's the last debate you had with someone?

399. When's the last time you condemned someone's behavior?

400. Did you ever follow someone around?

401. When's the last time you cut someone some slack?

402. Have you ever explained yourself to someone?

403. What's something you wish had been small instead of large?

404. Have you ever offered someone a way out of a situation?

405. Did you ever have a bad experience at the doctors?

406. Did you ever apply the "three strike rule" to your life?

407. How have you generated courage in the past?

408. Have you ever experienced something you thought was failure?

409. What's the longest distance you've ever traveled to see someone?

410. What's the last time someone stepped on your foot?

411. What was your experience during your last clinic visit?

412. Has anyone ever successfully mined for your emotions?

413. What was a battle you've won?

414. Have your expectations for someone ever been too high?

415. When's the last time you've had a fight or flight response?

416. Have you ever interacted with someone who was horrible?

417. Has anyone ever described you as "too green"?

418. Have you ever encountered someone who is too assertive?

419. Have you ever made a can and string phone?

420. When's the last time you got something delivered?

421. What's a prevalent trend in your adulthood?

422. Have you ever given yourself a haircut?

423. What have you always compartmentalized?

424. What's your favorite fiction story?

425. Who have you substituted in your life?

426. Have you ever swum in the ocean?

427. Would you go back to school?

428. What's a color you used to like or still looks good?

429. Who did you know that was bald and beautiful?

430. Have you ever given someone a glimpse into your life?

431. Have you ever witnessed a miracle?

432. Have you experienced flying in a helicopter?

433. What did you look forward to five years ago?

434. What did you look forward to ten years ago?

435. What's the formula to a great relationship?

436. What's the formula to a bad relationship?

437. Are you an empath?

438. Do you know how to draw?

439. Have you ever felt like you were paralyzed from fear?

440. What is your weapon of choice when fighting back?

441. Have you ever had a banner year?

442. Do you exercise often?

443. Who is the last person you've kissed on the lips?

444. What is information you should always have when traveling?

445. Do you treasure simplicity?

446. Does someone worry about you?

447. Has someone ever pampered you?

448. Have you ever been taken care of when sick?

449. What is something you picked up from someone else?

450. Have you ever had dental work done?

451. Can you roll your tongue?

452. Have you ever been fined for something?

453. Did you ever have recess?

454. Have you ever seen an explosion?

455. What's the most curated part of your life?

456. When's the last time you swam in a pool?

457. When's the last time you toasted someone?

458. When's the first time you ever said, "I love you"?

459. What's your go-to conversation starter?

460. When's the last time you went on a first date?

461. When's the last time you hung to someone's every word?

462. What's more important to you, speaking or listening?

463. Would you ever want to buy a house?

464. What do you prefer, a house or apartment?

465. What's in your library?

466. When's the last time you signed on the dotted line?

467. When do you know it's time to go?

468. Have you accepted something you think you didn't deserve?

469. Have you ever accepted something less than ideal?

470. What do you know you're not good at?

471. What's something someone said to you that changed your life?

472. What is an absolute truth?

473. Is it hard being the only one to do something?

474. Are you a meat lover?

475. Is there a confrontation you avoided for a while?

476. Do you know someone who was ever extorted?

477. Have you ever worn a real diamond?

478. Has there been a period of unrest in your life?

479. Do you remember the first pair of shoes you ever had?

480. Have you ever seen an artistic exhibition?

481. Make a chart showing your happiness over the last decade.

482. What did you think women wanted that you don't anymore?

483. What did you think men wanted that you don't anymore?

484. Function or beauty?

485. Is there a memory attached to your favorite song?

486. What is a definite no-no in your book?

487. What used to be your favorite board game?

488. How do you get all the toothpaste out of a tube?

489. Make a floorplan for what used to be your dreamhouse.

490. Who do you know that badly exaggerated a story?

491. What's a hit you were always willing to take?

492. How would you fare in a battlefield?

493. Do you have an ex?

494. What is your favorite payment method?

495. Has anything happened when all you've said is, "Unfortunate"?

496. What takes a toll on someone's body?

497. What takes a toll on someone's mind?

498. Have you ever been in a fist fight?

499. Are you into quaint or modern aesthetics?

500. What's an animal you're surprised is not extinct?

501. Have you ever burned out?

502. What activities do you not mind performing alone?

503. How do you feel when you do any of those activities?

504. If you could go anywhere, where would you travel?

505. Is there a place you have no interest in visiting?

506. What's the biggest secret you've kept for someone else?

507. Is there something you can always be objective about?

THE
PRESENT
IS A
PRESENT

"I was within and without, simultaneously enchanted and repelled by the inexhaustible variety of life."

—FITZGERALD F. SCOTT

508. What's the biggest secret you've kept from someone?

509. Who is your favorite family member?

510. Would you rather be somewhere else?

511. What are you noticing most about your current surroundings?

512. Do you foresee feeling gratitude at any point today?

513. What's the first thing you do when you feel angry?

514. What's the first thing you do when you feel sad?

515. Look around: what are five things you've never noticed before?

516. What's your favorite part of a hike in the forest?

517. What would you want a ton of in this moment?

518. Is there something you do to offset feelings of nervousness?

519. What is your conscience telling you?

520. Who is the most agile person you know?

521. Who would you choose if you could reconcile with one person?

522. Do you cry when you chop an onion?

523. Does finance stress you out?

524. What's important to you today that wasn't yesterday?

525. Which meal are you looking forward to today?

526. Do you review and reflect on your day before you go to bed?

527. What's the last coarse material you felt? Where and what was it?

528. If you could teleport anywhere, where would you go?

529. What's a commitment you could make right now?

530. Have you ever cried in front of someone?

531. If you had an emotional accountant, how would they advise you?

532. Who would you place in your personal board of directors?

533. Is there anything bothering you today?

534. Has someone ever called you a liar?

535. If you were able to be alone, what would you do?

536. If a crisis occurred right now, how would you react?

537. What's something you've only began to scratch the surface of?

538. When's the last time you saw something topple over?

539. What dictates your mood?

540. What do you consider to be abnormal?

541. Who is the most grounded person you know?

542. Who is the most scattered-brain person you know?

543. If you could make one thing disappear, what would it be?

544. Do you consider yourself street smart or book smart?

545. What fuels you today?

546. What are you looking for?

547. What scares you in this moment?

548. What are some of the things you can live without?

549. How do you feel when you depend on someone?

550. What's in the road in front of you?

551. What do you think of when you focus on your breath?

552. When's the last time you walked out of a room?

553. Who's on your speed dial?

554. What's a word that would describe your current environment?

555. Is there currently an ambiguous presence in your life?

556. What is rare for you?

557. Are you yearning for anything?

558. Is there someone nearby that you would consider calling noble?

559. Who is in your clique?

560. Who do you want to hug in this very moment?

561. Who do you admire most?

562. Why do you admire this person?

563. What was the last email you received?

564. What do you think will be your perception of life?

565. Are you in love?

566. Do you look your age?

567. Do you act your age?

568. How do you think you've developed as a human being?

569. Who do you think admires you?

570. If you could meet your parallel-universe self, would you?

571. Who would you give an award to for immeasurable support?

572. Do you wonder what it's like to be a teenager nowadays?

573. What is a tradition you always look forward to?

574. Is there a responsibility you wish you could shirk?

575. What do you think is the easiest job in the world?

576. What is making you proud?

577. What are you currently wearing?

578. Why did you choose what you're wearing at the moment?

579. What do you see when you look in the mirror?

580. What was something you changed your mind about?

581. What's the first thing you see when you leave home?

582. What do you want to be known for?

583. What is one thing you do to help you sleep?

584. What do you think is the hardest job in the world?

585. What happened the last time you smiled at someone?

586. When would you use a "Do Not Disturb" sign?

587. Who is the last person you had dinner with?

588. When was the last time you fought back tears?

589. What are you most concerned about at this very moment?

590. What is the worst apology you've ever heard?

591. What have you complained about today?

592. What are you looking forward to?

593. Have you told a lie today?

594. What is one hobby you've always wanted to get into?

595. Can you describe the photograph nearest to you?

596. Who in your immediate family would be a great president?

597. What's the last thing you've learned?

598. Are you replaying a situation in your head?

599. What's the last thing you've binge-watched?

600. Have you lost something recently?

601. Have your intentions ever been questioned?

602. When's the last time you opened the door for someone?

603. If you could make anything right now, what would it be?

604. Is there someone you've not been friendly toward?

605. Who was the last person you hugged?

606. Have you ever meditated?

607. What are the virtues of being street vs book smart?

608. What do you do when you feel lonely?

609. Have you told someone they mean a lot to you?

610. When was the last time you went outside?

611. Have you ever stood outside in the rain on purpose?

612. If you could free yourself from something, what would it be?

613. What is an act of generosity you can do?

614. Do you know someone you consider to be complicated?

615. Who would you miss terribly if they weren't around?

616. Who do you know that has the most beautiful eyes?

617. Is there someone in your life that criticizes you often?

618. Who is the funniest person you know?

619. Are you currently devoted to something?

620. What book are you currently reading?

621. Is today a lazy day?

622. What's a pattern you've noticed lately?

623. Have you ever just wandered around aimlessly and enjoyed it?

624. Can you remember a time you were extremely present?

625. Eastern medicine or Western medicine?

626. Do you have a title?

627. Have you ever had a title?

628. Are you a good card player?

629. Do titles mean anything to you?

630. What's something that every organization should have?

631. What background noise are you hearing right now?

632. Is the current background noise annoying you or soothing you?

633. What's a serial killer story that scares you?

634. What are your personal guidelines when you meet someone new?

635. Are you currently tiptoeing around someone's feelings? Why?

636. What usually brings a surge of energy to your day?

637. Do you think you could ever be a hunter-gatherer?

638. What's a public initiative you're impressed by?

639. What deters you from doing something erratic?

640. Who do you think needs rescuing in your life?

641. What's the glue that holds your family together?

642. What causes anxiety for you?

643. Do you enjoy being a tourist?

644. Do you place profit above other things?

645. When you disagree with someone how do you show it?

646. Do you always need to be in control?

647. Is there something you're not in control of right now?

648. What is entertainment for you that won't be for others?

649. Is there an art to dialogue?

650. Is there something you want to confess to?

651. Have you ever wanted to be a professional athlete?

652. What's a life strategy you wish more people implemented?

653. What should be a college requirement but isn't?

654. Have you ever gained perspective from someone's hurtful actions?

655. When's the last time you vegged out on the sofa?

656. Do you recall a time when you suffered from apathy?

657. What's a bargain you can't ever resist?

658. Have you ever made a mixtape?

659. What's in your drawer in this moment?

660. Have you ever had your heart broken?

661. How do you remain focused?

662. What will always belong to you no matter what?

663. What's the fairest decision you've seen someone make?

664. When's the last time you spilled secrets?

665. Have you ever prayed for something specific?

666. Who is your favorite flawed character?

667. Have you ever swum underneath a waterfall?

668. Do you feel like you're ordinary?

669. What's the last item you got a refund for?

670. Do you have a bucket list?

671. Have you ever fought someone over compensation?

672. When's the last time you went to the hospital?

673. How direct are you with other people?

674. Are you a runner?

675. Does the moon hold special meaning for you?

676. Have you ever been closed off to someone?

677. Have you ever felt helpless?

678. Are you an orthodox person?

679. Does someone represent your ideals?

680. When have you demonstrated vigorous discipline?

681. Have you ever been on the hook for something?

682. Do you have a memory of crossing a street by yourself?

683. How happy are you in this moment?

684. Who would you tell that they mean the world to you?

685. How have you closed the gap between you and another?

686. Where are your ancestors from?

687. Have you ever held on to hope against the odds?

688. Do you like reading poetry?

689. Have you noticed someone trying hard and not succeeding?

690. Have you ridden the subway?

691. Imagine only being on this earth with one other person.

692. Are you extremely faithful to your autonomy?

693. Do you believe you have good instincts?

694. What is something you wrongly thought was useless?

695. How much does it frustrate you to untangle a wire?

696. How do you diffuse tension?

697. Have you ever been the member of a club?

698. What do your clothes say about you?

699. Do you consider yourself to be a loyal person?

700. Have you ever seen someone reveal a part of themselves?

701. Do you consider your bathroom a sanctuary?

702. When's the last time you used a hammer?

703. Have you ever used a cane?

704. Does technology distract?

705. How knowledgeable are you about your family's history?

706. How do you like your eggs in the morning?

707. When's the last time you sang out loud?

708. What do you think about when you think about your family?

709. When is the last time you cried?

710. Is there an impulse you have at this very moment?

711. Are you currently in control of your finances?

712. When's the last time you honked at another driver?

713. Do you extend kindness to everyone or only some people?

714. Do you embarrass easily?

715. When's the last time you felt velvet?

716. What have you done out of spite?

717. Is it important for people to have credibility?

718. Are you a good person to brainstorm with?

719. Do you usually let laundry get out of hand?

720. Have you ever had to recover from something?

721. Do you enjoy staying in?

722. What is your relationship with your parents?

723. Do you have a vivid memory on a street corner?

724. What is a wise gem of knowledge you've read recently?

725. Are you a good cook?

726. When's the last time you felt immense relief?

727. Have you ever willingly admitted defeat?

728. What's your favorite herb to cook with?

729. Have you ever guaranteed something to someone?

730. Do you admire people who are fashionable?

731. Do you think you've ever broken someone's heart?

732. Do you let your inhibitions hold you back?

733. Have you made a premature decision you regret?

734. Is your hair meaningful to you?

735. How health-conscious are you?

736. Have you been unaware of someone having a crush on you?

737. Who have you ever made a formal complaint about? Why?

738. When is the last time you lit a candle?

739. Have you ever made a New Year's resolution?

740. Have you ever been the designated driver?

741. What is the worst story you have of a car ride?

742. Have you ever carpooled with strangers?

743. Have you ever been in love with two people simultaneously?

744. Who would you trust with a power of attorney?

745. Have you ever said something you had to take back?

746. Do you think being picky about food is a fault?

747. Who requires a lot of patience from you?

748. Who are you always learning from?

749. What is a label you would wear proudly?

750. Have you ever wanted to kiss someone?

751. What does youth mean to you?

752. Is there something you regret?

753. Where do you see yourself in five years?

754. When is the last time you remember laughing uncontrollably?

755. Which of your five senses do you value the most?

756. What's your all-time favorite movie?

757. What's the one luxury you wish were everywhere?

LOOKING FORWARD TO THE FUTURE

"Live! Live the wonderful life that is in you! Let nothing be lost upon you. Be always searching for new sensations. Be afraid of nothing."

—OSCAR WILDE

758. What does your dream house look like?

759. How would you change the world?

760. What do you think about in terms of a future family?

761. Do you get overwhelmed planning the future?

762. When you were younger, what career did you want?

763. What is the first thing you're going to do tomorrow?

764. What are your hopes and dreams?

765. What's a fantasy you revisit constantly?

766. What is the one thing you should always have?

767. If you were to negotiate a contract, what are the terms?

768. What's the best kind of emotional investment?

769. If you could name an avenue, what name would you choose?

770. If a designer could style you, who would you choose?

771. What do you think about when you get dressed?

772. What's the first rule you would enact as a principal?

773. How would you want warring nations to settle their differences?

774. What do you think is infinite?

775. If you had the option to change jobs, would you?

776. How would you want people to describe how your life progressed?

777. If you could stand in onstage, what would you perform?

778. What should a place you shelter in always have?

779. How would you like to better approach confrontation?

780. Is there a photograph you wish would never fade?

781. Do you feel you're on the edge of something great?

782. Who could always call you and you'd hangout with right away?

783. What is a sound that brings you great comfort?

784. What do you do when you feel lazy?

785. What do you prefer, email, text, or a phone call?

786. If you could, would you carry a camera everywhere?

787. What's the one thing you could lose and wouldn't care about?

788. Do you think your definition of loyalty will change?

789. Where do you see yourself in ten years?

790. When you're still, what do you think about?

791. Have you ever speculated about someone's life?

792. What are two things you wish you had?

793. Is there anything you would change about school?

794. What is the best way to deal with grief?

795. Do you believe you have to push people to be great?

796. What do you observe in people that makes them likeable?

797. Are you someone who would push the button?

798. Is there something you would never discourage someone to do?

799. What would you take to a desolate island?

800. What is a characteristic of a perfect parent?

801. What is a characteristic of a perfect grandparent?

802. What do you want people to always say about you?

803. Are you careful with your words?

804. Who was the last person that told you to calm down?

805. When is the last time a smell triggered a memory?

806. What is something you think should be limited?

807. What is the one thing you know is unattainable?

808. Have you ever wanted to learn an instrument?

809. What's life's prominent variable?

810. What does an ideal world look like to you?

811. When's the last time you were by the ocean?

812. If you were a salesperson, what would you sell?

813. Is there something that you don't want to be afraid of?

814. What is something you would do anything to get?

815. What's something you always do now that you never did before?

816. If you could invent anything, what would it be?

817. Do you know someone who is the best spouse?

818. If you could live someone else's life, who would it be?

819. Where do you see yourself in twenty years?

820. What is something someone can always find in your home?

821. What of yours would you include in a time capsule?

822. Who would you give a eulogy for?

823. What is the one thing everyone should know?

824. What do you want your legacy to be?

825. If you ever wrote a book, what would you name it?

826. What is something you wish you could collect?

827. What has worked for you when making decisions?

828. What is an indication of a good friend?

829. What's something you would do if you won the lottery?

830. What do you think about ageing?

831. Who is the best giver and taker in your life?

832. Would you ever get plastic surgery?

833. What do you envision when you see yourself getting older?

834. What is the one thing you always save?

835. Where do you see yourself in thirty years?

836. What makes a good marriage?

837. What makes a bad marriage?

838. Do you believe in quality over quantity?

839. What's the last text message you received?

840. Do you think about the future often?

841. What advice do you have for your younger self?

842. Who is someone you would want to give your eulogy?

843. What's a story you're always going to tell once you're old?

844. Could you ever live as a minimalist?

845. Are you always aware of other's feelings?

846. Do you think you could ever give up your favorite food?

847. Would you dye your hair if it's too gray?

848. What is the one thing you will always keep private?

849. What is a secret that you will always keep?

850. If you could heal someone, who would it be?

851. Do you think someone must have a legacy?

852. Have you ever considered how you can change the world?

853. How do your decisions affect others?

854. Are there people in your life that you want to connect?

855. Do you tend to let people get away with things?

856. If you could start your own business, what would it be?

857. Which celebrity would you trade places with?

858. Who will always have the power to break your heart?

859. Do you think there is power in being vulnerable?

860. How do you measure success?

861. When's the last time you experienced performance anxiety?

862. What's the last list you made?

863. Who in your life is a "knight in shining armor"?

864. What physical items would you store away right now?

865. What emotions would you store away at this very moment?

866. What are three wishes you would ask a genie for?

867. If you were offered immortality, would you take it?

868. What are three bad habits you dislike seeing in others?

869. What does a family look like to you?

870. What would someone say if they were to introduce you?

871. How would someone describe your life's journey?

872. Who has a part of your soul?

873. Have you ever told someone you needed them?

874. Do you think extra pounds are a bad thing?

875. What kind of houseguest are you?

876. Are you concerned a lot with fairness?

877. How much of an observer are you?

878. Do you ask for help when you need to?

879. Sunblock or suntan lotion?

880. Who is company that you won't ever mind having around?

881. Who deserves a medal for all they do?

882. Where do you see yourself tomorrow?

883. What's the one think you couldn't conceive ever happening?

884. Is there something you'd eventually like to defeat?

885. Do you think there's an unconscious bias in you?

886. What's the one thing you will always put effort toward?

887. What is something you believe in wholeheartedly?

888. Is there a video you will always want to watch?

889. What is your number one rational fear?

890. Who would you give all your money to?

891. If you could choose your future, how would it be?

892. Do you see yourself having an office job in the future?

893. What five people would you invite to dinner?

894. If you could have one superpower, what would it be?

895. Are there people you know who look down on you?

896. Who's the one family member you'd never ask for help?

897. Have you ever asked someone for a loan?

898. What would you want your very last meal to be?

899. How do you measure someone's goodness?

900. Have you ever smoked a cigarette?

901. How do you feel about opera?

902. Who do you always give the benefit of the doubt to?

903. Who do you feel safest with?

904. Is there something you fear you will never outgrow?

905. What do you believe is the best thing about being a human?

906. How do you measure your days?

907. What's a priority for you today?

908. Who will you give a compliment to today?

909. Do you believe in always keeping it short and sweet?

910. What would be your million-dollar idea?

911. Do you have a good memory?

912. What fuels you when you're down?

913. What do you think science will do in your lifetime?

914. When's the last time you went out to dance?

915. If you were to get a chest tattoo, what would it be?

916. Who was the last person you asked permission from?

917. When's the last time you wrote a letter?

918. What is unreasonable to you?

919. What's your version of modern-day battle gear?

920. What is the most effective way to communicate?

921. Have you tried to be more involved in your community?

922. What always kills your concentration?

923. Have you ever made a prediction that made you sad?

924. What's your favorite expression to use?

925. What is the best version of yourself?

926. Do you believe in regret?

927. What's a competition you would do really well in?

928. Have you taken a road off the beaten path?

929. Have you ever had your palm read?

930. When is the last time you said, "You're right"?

931. Could you say you've wrestled your demons?

932. Have you ever held a grudge toward someone?

933. What isn't a crime but should be?

934. Who do you know that has made a significant improvement?

935. Whose approval do you seek?

936. What is your definition of relaxation?

937. What will always be comedy to you?

938. What do you always have in your bag?

939. Who is the last person you told to calm down?

940. What button would you wear proudly?

941. What is your word?

942. What happened the last time you had a fever?

943. What is cruel to you but not to other people?

944. What's the last drink you had?

945. What's the last great gesture you made?

946. Have you ever been punched? What happened?

947. What is something you look for when you're gift-giving?

948. What's a stereotype you've lived up to?

949. What is something you would trade away in a heartbeat?

950. What has captivated your attention recently?

951. Are you the person to call in an emergency?

952. When was the last time you whispered?

953. Do you believe politics is a public service?

954. What was discussed at the last meeting you attended?

955. Have you ever translated a document?

956. Lemonade or limeade?

957. If you could take a drive anywhere, where would it be?

958. Have you ever despised anyone? Why?

959. What's a mystery you wish you could solve?

960. What's a message you share with everyone?

961. When was the last time you broke a sweat?

962. What is your favorite seasonal transition?

963. If you could have multiple professions, which would they be?

964. Have you ever tried to replace someone in your heart?

965. How would you describe an emotional recession?

966. If you could be immune to one thing, what would it be?

967. Do you equate growth with maturity?

968. Where can you go for some peace and quiet?

969. What is the best way someone can show they care?

970. When's the last time you've been on a slide?

971. What's a struggle you would always choose?

972. How do you divide your days?

973. Who would you consider to be your arch nemesis?

974. How do you spend the majority of your day?

975. Who's come into your life to shake things up?

976. Has there ever been a casualty from your indecision?

977. Have you ever shot a rifle?

978. Have you ever rolled your ankle?

979. Name all the eras of your life.

980. What's a giant leap you've taken?

981. If you were a category, what would it be?

982. Has anyone ever tried to distort your words?

983. Should protection be a right or a luxury?

984. Who's the best performer you know?

985. Are you a night owl?

986. Who do you always take for consideration?

987. What should be the penalty for rudeness?

988. What would the first page of your book contain?

989. What's the highest temperature you've ever experienced?

990. What's the last celebration you attended?

991. Build your own "make my dream come true" kit.

992. Do you believe even your acquaintances should be good company?

993. Would someone describe you as talented?

994. What can you always tell from a person's handshake?

995. How do you honor your body?

996. Is it ever too late to do what makes you feel purposeful?

997. Can you tell when someone is lying?

998. What does honor mean to you?

999. Who do you always have great chemistry with?

1000. Has someone ever tried to rescue you?

1001. How do you prioritize the things that matter most?

Inspiring | Educating | Creating | Entertaining

Brimming with creative inspiration, how-to projects, and useful information to enrich your everyday life, quarto.com is a favorite destination for those pursuing their interests and passions.

First published in 2021 by Chartwell Books,
an imprint of The Quarto Group,
142 West 36th Street, 4th Floor,
New York, NY 10018 USA
T (212) 779-4972 F (212) 779-6058
www.Quarto.com

Chartwell titles are also available at discount for retail, wholesale, promotional, and bulk purchase. For details, contact the Special Sales Manager by email at specialsales@quarto.com or by mail at The Quarto Group, Attn: Special Sales Manager, 100 Cummings Center Suite 265D, Beverly, MA 01915, USA.

10 9 8 7 6 5 4

ISBN: 978-0-7858-3961-3

Publisher: Rage Kindelsperger
Creative Director: Laura Drew
Managing Editor: Cara Donaldson
Editorial Assistant: Yashu Pericherla
Cover and Interior Design: Beth Middleworth

Printed in China